The Boy Who Cried Wolf

Retold by Lucy Lawrence
Illustrated by Chantal Stewart

Once upon a time, there was a young shepherd boy who lived in a small village. Each morning, the boy took the sheep along a path, over the hill, and down to the edge of the forest where the grass was greenest.

Each day, the sheep grazed quietly, and there was very little for the boy to do. He felt bored and lonely, and he would have liked to run off and find someone to play with. But his father had always told him, "You must stay close to the sheep. There are hungry wolves in the forest, and they are always looking for a nice fat sheep for dinner."

So the boy sat with his back against a tree, wishing for something exciting to happen to make his job more interesting. Sometimes he almost wished that a wolf *would* come out of the forest.

One day, he had an idea. The sheep were grazing quietly, and, as usual, there was not a wolf in sight. But suddenly the boy shouted at the top of his voice: **"Wolf! Wolf! A wolf is taking one of the sheep!"**

Back in the village the people heard the boy's cries. They ran as fast as they could over the hill and down to the edge of the forest, hoping that they would get there in time to save the sheep from being eaten.

When they got there, of course, there was no wolf in sight. The villagers counted the sheep and found every single one of them safe and sound.

"Did you *really* see a wolf?" the villagers asked the shepherd boy.

"Oh yes," he said, "but it ran back into the forest."

The villagers wondered whether the boy was telling the truth, but they stayed for a while, just in case, to make sure that no wolves were about.

The boy thought that his trick had worked very well. He liked having so many visitors, and the rest of the day passed quickly.

he next day, and the next day after that, the boy took the sheep over the hill and down to the edge of the forest as usual. Each day, the sheep grazed quietly, and soon the boy grew as lonely and bored as before.

So on the third day, he decided to play his trick again. Taking a deep breath, he shouted: **"Wolf! Wolf! A wolf is taking one of the sheep!"**

Back in the village the people heard the boy's cries, and they ran as quickly as they could to help him.

When they got there, of course, there was no wolf in sight. The villagers looked at one another doubtfully, and then, once again, they asked the shepherd boy, "Did you *really* see a wolf?"

"Oh yes," said the boy, "but it ran away through the tall grass."

This time the villagers were almost certain that the boy had played a trick on them, but they stayed for a while, just in case, to make sure that no wolves were about. The boy was pleased that his trick had worked so well.

The next day, and the next day after that, the boy took the sheep over the hill and down to the edge of the forest as usual.

Each day, the sheep grazed quietly.

But on the third day, just as the boy was wondering whether he would play his trick again, out of the forest there crept . . . **a hungry wolf!**

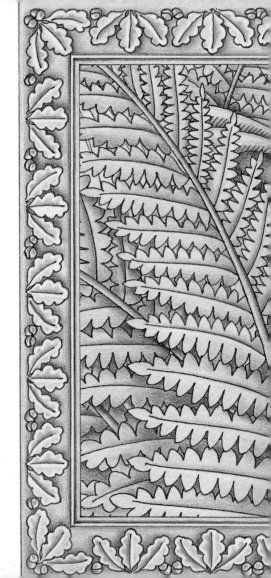

It prowled around the flock, looking for a nice fat sheep for dinner.

The sheep began to *baa* nervously, and the boy, who had been daydreaming about his friends back in the village, looked up with a start.

Seeing the wolf crouching at the edge of the flock, licking its lips with its wet red tongue, he jumped up in alarm and shouted: **"Wolf! Wolf!"**

Just then, the wolf chose the fattest sheep and pounced. It took hold of the thick wool, and tried to drag the sheep away.

The boy cried out louder than ever: **"Wolf! Wolf! A wolf is taking one of the sheep!"**

Back in the village the people heard the boy's cries. But this time they didn't run to help. They stayed right where they were and said to each other, "Ha! There isn't really a wolf. The shepherd boy won't trick us this time!"

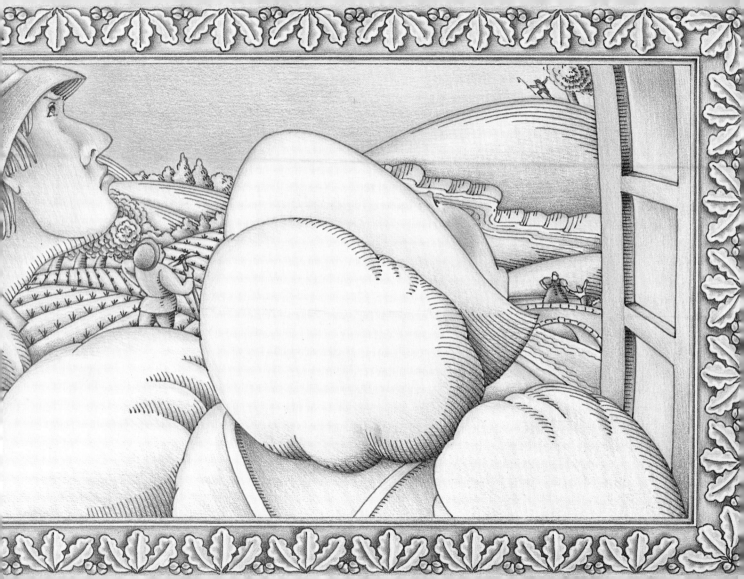

The boy felt very frightened when he realized that no one was coming to help him, but he knew that he had to act quickly. "Let go! Let go!" he cried as he ran toward the wolf. Then he grabbed the sheep, and tugged with all his might.

The startled wolf tugged too, but all it got was a mouthful of wool, while the boy was left with the wounded sheep in his arms.

He carried the sheep all the way back to the village, while the rest of the frightened flock scurried along behind him.

"See what the wolf has done!" cried the boy. "Why didn't you come to help?"

"You called us twice before when there was *no* wolf," said the villagers. "How could we believe you this time?"

The shepherd boy's face went red. He knew that he was to blame. "I only played tricks because I was lonely," he said quietly.

"Well, I hope that you have learned a lesson," said the boy's father. "And because you saved the sheep all by yourself, I will see if I can find you a friend to keep you company."

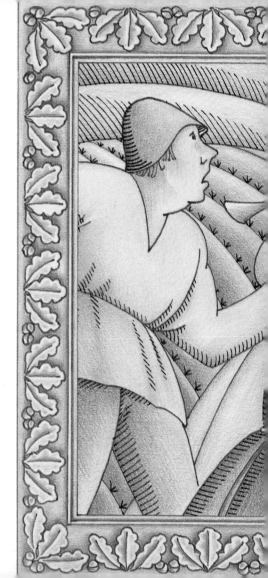

The next morning, the boy took the
sheep out of the village as usual, but
this time he had a special new friend
trotting beside him.

From that day on, the boy looked after
the sheep without feeling lonely.
And he grew up to be a very fine
shepherd — and a very honest man.

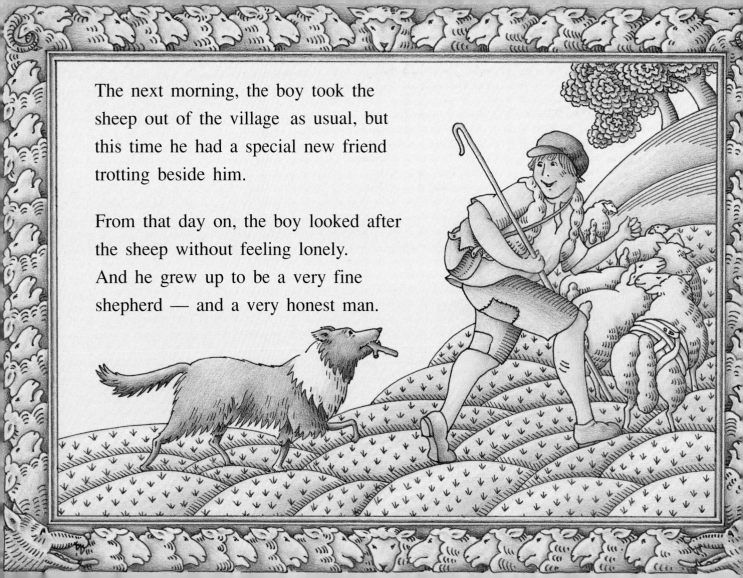